# Cranbury Public Library

23 North Main St., Cranbury, NJ 08512
(609) 655-0555   f: (609) 655-2858

www.CranburyPublicLibrary.org

# At a
# Picnic

by **Dana Meachen Rau**

Reading Consultant: Nanci R. Vargus, Ed.D.

**Marshall Cavendish**
Benchmark
New York

# Picture Words

 ants

 blanket

 book

 frogs

 grass

 net

 picnic

 pond

 rocks

 tree

 watermelon

We like to go on a .

We sit in the .

We toss  in a .

8

We pick up  with
a 🔴.

We read a on
the .

We play hide-and-seek behind a .

We eat .

We see 🐜🐜🐜🐜.

We have fun on a .

## Words to Know

**hide**   to go where no one can see you

**seek**   to look for something

**toss**   to throw something lightly

# Find Out More

## Books

Dahl, Michael. *Ants at the Picnic:Counting by Tens*. Minneapolis, MN: Picture Window Books, 2006.

Goode, Diane. *The Most Perfect Spot*. New York: HarperCollins, 2006.

Williams, David K. *Green Light Readers: The Picnic*. New York: Harcourt, 2006.

## Videos

Gordon, Tom. *See How They Grow: Pond Animals*. Sony Kids' Video.

## Web Sites

**Games Kids Play**
http://www.gameskidsplay.net/

**Simple Kids' Picnic Recipes**
http://www.picnicportal.com/simple-kids-picnic-recipes.htm

## About the Author

Dana Meachen Rau is an author, editor, and illustrator. A graduate of Trinity College in Hartford, Connecticut, she has written more than one hundred books for children, including nonfiction, biographies, early readers, and historical fiction. She likes to go on picnics with her family in Burlington, Connecticut, where they eat peanut butter and marshmallow sandwiches.

## About the Reading Consultant

Nanci R. Vargus, Ed.D., wants all children to enjoy reading. She used to teach first grade. Now she works at the University of Indianapolis. Nanci helps young people become teachers. She likes to canoe on Sugar Creek and stop for a picnic lunch along the beach.

Marshall Cavendish Benchmark
99 White Plains Road
Tarrytown, NY 10591-9001
www.marshallcavendish.us

Library of Congress Cataloging-in-Publication Data

Rau, Dana Meachen, 1971–
At a picnic / Dana Meachen Rau ; reading consultant, Nanci R. Vargus.
    p. cm. — (Benchmark Rebus)
Summary: "Easy to read text with rebuses explores fun activities at a picnic"—Provided by publisher.
Includes bibliographical references.
ISBN-13: 978-0-7614-2607-3
1. Picnicking—Juvenile literature. 2. Rebuses. I. Vargus, Nanci Reginelli. II. Title. III. Series.
GT2955.R38 2007
394'.3—dc22        2006030808

Editor: Christine Florie
Publisher: Michelle Bisson
Art Director: Anahid Hamparian
Series Designer: Virginia Pope

Photo research by Connie Gardner

Rebus images provided courtesy of *Dorling Kindersley*.

Cover photo by Mark E.Gibson/Dembinsky Photo Associates

*Getty Images*: p. 5, Taxi; p.15, The Image Bank; *Jupiter Images*: p. 7, Stock Image; p. 9, Agence Images; p.11, Index Stock Imagery; *Corbis*: p. 13, Roy Morsch; p. 19, Awilli/zefa; p. 21, Grace/zefa; *The Image Works*: p. 17, Ellen B. Senisi.

Printed in Malaysia
1  3  5  6  4  2